WILD WICKED WONDERFUL

TOP 10:

SUPER SENSES

By Virginia Loh-Hagan

45th Parallel Press

Published in the United States of America by Cherry Lake Publishing
Ann Arbor, Michigan
www.cherrylakepublishing.com

Content Adviser: Stephen Ditchkoff, Professor of Wildlife Ecology and Management, Auburn University, Alabama
Reading Adviser: Marla Conn MS, Ed., Literacy specialist, Read-Ability, Inc.
Book Designer: Melinda Millward

Photo Credits: © Khoroshunova Olga/Shutterstock.com, cover, 1, 6; © Jurriaan Huting/iStockphoto, 5; © mosista/Shutterstock.com, 6; © Ondrej Prosicky/Shutterstock.com, 6; © Efired/Shutterstock.com, 7; © E R DEGGINGER / Getty Images, 8; © Mary Gascho/iStockphoto, 8; © blickwinkel / Alamy Stock Photo, 8; © FLPA/Dembinsky Photo / Getty Images, 9; © Eduard Kyslynskyy/Shutterstock.com, 10; © Matthew J Thomas/Shutterstock.com, 10; © Karelian/Shutterstock.com, 10; © Frederic Prochasson/iStockphoto, 11; © plastique/Shutterstock.com, 12; © Manfred Ruckszio/Shutterstock.com, 12; © Jim Parkin/Shutterstock.com, 12; © Igor Normann/Shutterstock.com, 13; © deepspace/Shutterstock.com, 14; © Bildagentur Zoonar GmbH/Shutterstock.com, 16; © Katarina Christenson/Shutterstock.com, 16; © teptong/iStockphoto, 16; © Steven Ellingson/Shutterstock.com, 17; © Gilitukha/iStockphoto, 18; © alenas/Shutterstock.com, 18; © Peter Betts/Shutterstock.com, 18; © Pearl Media/Shutterstock.com, 19; © Ruthie44/Dreamstime.com, 20; © NatureLovePhotography/Thinkstock, 20; © avs_lt /iStockphoto, 20; © Tory Kallman/Shutterstock.com, 21; © outdoorsman/Shutterstock.com, 22; © Mark Kostich/iStockphoto, 22; © beejung/Shutterstock.com, 22; © Dennis W Donohue/Shutterstock.com, 23; © Eterovic/Dreamstime.com, 24; © vladoskan/Thinkstock, 26; © worldswildlifewonders/Shutterstock.com, 26; © Olga Demchishina/iStockphoto, 26; © Albert Lleal / Getty Images, 27; © FishTales/Thinkstock, 28; © Fufachew Ivan Andreevich/Shutterstock.com, 29; © Whitepointer/Dreamstime.com, 30; © Elsa Hoffmann/Shutterstock.com, 30; © VisionDive/Shutterstock.com, 30; © Photomyeye/Dreamstime.com, 31

Graphic Element Credits: ©tukkki/Shutterstock.com, back cover, front cover, multiple interior pages; ©paprika/Shutterstock.com, back cover, front cover, multiple interior pages; ©Silhouette Lover/Shutterstock.com, multiple interior pages

45th Parallel Press is an imprint of Cherry Lake Publishing.

Library of Congress Cataloging-in-Publication Data

Names: Loh-Hagan, Virginia, author.
Title: Top 10—super senses / by Virginia Loh-Hagan.
Description: Ann Arbor : Cherry Lake Publishing, 2017. | Series: Extreme animals/wild wicked wonderful |
    Includes bibliographical references and index.
Identifiers: LCCN 2016031168| ISBN 9781634721417 | ISBN 9781634722070 |
    ISBN 9781634722735 | ISBN 9781634723398
Subjects: LCSH: Senses and sensation—Juvenile literature. | Animals—Juvenile literature.
Classification: LCC QP434 .L64 2017 | DDC 612.8—dc23
LC record available at https://lccn.loc.gov/2016031168

Printed in the United States of America
Corporate Graphics

About the Author

Dr. Virginia Loh-Hagan is an author, university professor, former classroom teacher, and curriculum designer. She has a super sense for eating bad food and buying pianos. She lives in San Diego with her very tall husband and very naughty dogs. To learn more about her, visit www.virginialoh.com.

TABLE OF CONTENTS

INTRODUCTION

Animals use their senses. They see. They smell. They hear. They feel. They taste.

They **survive**. Survive means to live. They live in the wild. They have to be smart. They use their skills. They use their senses. They adapt to their **habitats**. Habitats are where they live.

Some animals live in extreme habitats. They developed super senses. They have super vision. They have super hearing. They have extraordinary abilities. Their senses are special. They're beyond normal. These animals have the most exciting super senses in the animal world!

Animals need senses to help them survive.

Chapter one

TARSIERS

Tarsiers live in Southeast Asia. They're small animals. But they have really big eyes. Their eyes are as big as their brain. Their skull helps them balance their big eyes and heavy head. Tarsiers can't move their eyes. Their eyes are fixed in their skulls. They have to turn their heads to see. They can turn their heads 180 degrees.

Big eyes let in more light. Tarsiers have great night vision. They hunt. They see **prey** 20 feet (6 meters) away. Prey are animals hunted for food. Tarsiers can leap over 20 times their body length. They land with accuracy. They attack.

Tarsiers also have good hearing.
They can hear high-pitched sounds.

chapter two

STAR-NOSED MOLES

Star-nosed moles live in dark tunnels. They can't see. They feel their way in the dark. They have a special **snout**. A snout is a projecting nose and mouth. Their snout has 22 fleshy **appendages**. Appendages are like fingers. They're very sensitive. They're always moving.

Their appendages have over 25,000 touch **receptors**. Receptors are like feelers. They detect tiny movements in the soil. They feel prey move. They identify prey by touch.

Star-nosed moles' appendages are called rays.

Star-nosed moles can eat lots of bugs at once. Their
appendages can sense many prey in the area. They
also keep dirt from entering their nose.

Chapter three

PIGS

Pigs have a large head. They have a long snout. Their snout has a special bone. It has a special muscle at the tip. The snouts are strong. Pigs dig with it. They dig better. They find food faster. They also have a strong sense of smell.

Pigs have super tasting skills. Their tongue has over 15,000 taste buds. That's three times more than human tongues. There was a study. Pigs rejected 171 out of 200 vegetables. They're picky eaters. They taste different flavors.

Pigs are highly social and intelligent animals.

Pigs are **omnivores**. They eat plants and meat. They prefer **savory** to sweet. Savory is salty or spicy. They know when food is healthy or unhealthy.

chapter four
DOGS

Dogs smell very well. They have a long snout. They have more room for receptors. They have about 220 million receptors. Their snout is super sensitive. Their snout has bones. These bones help them smell. This allows dogs to detect **faint** odors. Faint means not strong.

Dogs have special tissue in their brain. It's located in the front of the brain. It processes smells detected by the nose. Humans have this tissue, too. But it's 40 times larger in dogs than humans. It's one-eighth of a dog's brain.

The olfactory bulb is a bulb of neural tissue within the dog's brain.

Smelling is the most important sense for dogs. It's developed from birth. Other senses develop later.

Dogs detect odors about 100,000 times better than humans.

Dogs smell things humans can't. They detect feelings. They detect sicknesses. They detect drugs. They detect bombs.

Dogs recognize different smells. Their noses move. Their wet noses trap smells. This helps them remember.

Dogs like to roll around. They roll in stinky things. They hide their scent. This lets them sneak up on prey.

Dogs sniff other dogs. They sniff to mate. They sniff to make friends. They leave messages with smells. They pee. They poop. Their waste has smells. Male dogs mark their **territory** with waste. Territory is area.

Humans Do What?!?

Some humans have super noses. Dr. Michael Levitt is a stomach doctor. He's also an odor tester. He smells farts. Bad farts smell like "rotten eggs." It could mean a disease. Levitt worked with 16 healthy subjects. The subjects ate beans. Levitt trapped their fart gas. He put it in containers. He collected over 100 samples. Odor testers opened each container. They smelled the fart gas. They judged each smell. Human stomach smells are important. They're used to find health problems. Some Chinese people believe farts are important. Professional fart smellers are called *wen pishi*. This means "fart-sniffing master." Farts have different smells. They're bitter, savory, sweet, fishy, or meaty. Odor testers have good noses. They can't have any allergies. They can't have any breathing problems. They can't drink or smoke. Their noses have to be clean!

Chapter five
MOTHS

Female moths release smells into the air. They release a small amount. Males pick up the scent. They smell mates over 6 miles (9.6 kilometers) away. Females' scents get more faint over distances. But males still sniff them out.

Moths don't suck up smells likes noses do. Moths don't have noses. They have **antennae**. Antennae are feelers. Their antennae are like feathers. Males' antennae have 40,000 receptors. They help moths smell. Males use antennae to find females.

Moths have thick, hairy bodies and large wings.

Moths have other body parts with receptors. They have **setae**. Setae are hairs that sense things. Setae comb the air for scents.

Chapter six

ELEPHANTS

Elephants live in Africa and Asia. They have a **trunk**. Trunks are a combination of a nose and an upper lip. Trunks have many uses. They smell. They smell water several miles away. They smell water underground. They make sounds. Elephants talk to each other. They make many calls. They send sound waves that humans can't hear. Their sound waves bend around objects. Trunks touch. They touch faces. They stroke. They hug.

Elephants can hear well. They have the world's biggest ears. They detect sound waves. They use their feet. Their feet have nerves. They take in sounds.

Trunks have over 100,000 muscles.

Chapter seven

BOTTLENOSE DOLPHINS

Bottlenose dolphins live in the cold ocean. Dolphins' noses are **blowholes**. Blowholes are nostrils on top of their heads. Every few minutes, dolphins surface for air.

Their brains are bigger than a human brain! They use **echolocation** to see things. They have large fatty organs on their foreheads. They send out **ultrasound**. These are invisible sound waves. They listen to sounds bouncing off things. Their brain forms an image. It senses size, shape, and speed.

Dolphins have super hearing. They detect sounds humans

Bottlenose dolphins can recognize themselves in mirrors. Dolphins are one of the only animals that can do this.

can't hear. They listen to each other talk. They whistle and click. They make high-pitched sounds. They use air **sacs** below their blowholes. Sacs are bags. Each dolphin has its own special sound.

Chapter eight

SNAKES

Snakes are built to be great hunters. They track down prey. They hunt above ground. They hunt below ground. They hunt at night. They hunt during the day.

They have very strong senses. Pit vipers have pits on the sides of their faces. The pits see special light. The pits feel heat. The pits send information to the brain. This means nothing can hide. Snakes can see and feel prey. They also defend themselves. They bite things that get too close.

Snakes have a strong bite reflex.
They bite once. They bite quickly.

Snakes don't dance. They're feeling sound waves.

Snakes still bite after they die. Their pits feel heat for hours after death. This happens even if a snake's head gets chopped off. The head will keep biting. Its nerves still work.

Snakes taste the air. They use their tongue. This also helps them smell. Tongues trap scents. They carry scents to a special organ. This organ is in the mouth. It identifies scents as food or danger. The tongue is forked. This helps snakes figure out which side has the stronger smell. This helps them find their prey better.

Snakes can't hear. They feel movements in the ground. They have good eyesight. They see small movements.

DID YOU KNOW...?

- Tarsiers stress out easily. Stress causes them to kill themselves. They bash their heads against something. Then, they die.

- Star-nosed moles can smell underwater. They make air bubbles to breathe.

- Pigs have short, stiff, coarse hair called bristles. Their bristles have been used in paintbrushes.

- Sharks sometimes get their teeth stuck in what they bite. They lose and replace teeth.

- Dog bites are more dangerous than bites from bears, alligators, and spiders combined! Dog spit has germs. Victims could get rabies. Rabies is a bad sickness. It's killed over 55,000 people a year.

- Snake teeth can be found in their poop. They get stuck in prey. Snakes eat the prey. The teeth pass through their bodies.

- Aquariums won't take mantis shrimp because they kill other creatures in the tank. They can also break aquarium glass with a single strike!

Chapter nine

MANTIS SHRIMP

Mantis shrimp have powerful eyes. Their eyes are bigger than their brain. Their eyes make them strong hunters.

They have green eyes. Their eyes are on **stalks**. Stalks are like sticks. The stalks are on top of their head. They have antennae on their head. They see objects with three parts of the same eye. Nothing gets past them!

They see light and colors that humans can't see. They see 16 colors. Humans only see three colors. Mantis shrimp filter out colors they don't need. They can live in shallow and deep waters.

Mantis shrimp see colors for which we don't have names.

Mantis shrimp process information with their eyes. Humans process with their brain.

Mantis shrimp have complex eyes. They have a simple brain. So, they can't see shades. Humans see thousands of shades.

Mantis shrimp use their eyes to hunt. They use their powerful claws to kill. They slice through prey. Their claws move like a spring. They have the world's fastest strike.

They're mean. They're dangerous. They're **predators**. They stun prey. They tear them apart. They pull out their limbs. They also send out a shockwave. The shockwave slams into prey.

When Animals Attack!

Reindeer adapted to the Arctic's extreme snow. They can see ultraviolet light. There are only a few mammals that can. They also have a special nose. Their nose warms incoming cold air. They smell well. Pat Cook lives in the United Kingdom. A reindeer attacked her. Cook was walking in the hills. The reindeer got separated from its herd. It pounced on her. It knocked her to the ground. It attacked her for two hours. She said, "I grabbed the antlers to try and avoid getting stabbed, and it started to bump me along the ground." She fell. She lay still. The reindeer got distracted. She ran away. She said, "I tried to hurry to get out of its range of vision." She got bruises. She has trouble walking. But she survived.

chapter ten

GREAT WHITE SHARKS

Great white sharks are the largest predatory fish. They grow to 20 feet (6 m). They weigh 4,000 pounds (1,814 kilograms). They have a large amount of muscle.

They're great hunters. They find prey easily. They have super eyesight. Their eyes are super sensitive to light. They have super hearing. They hear prey a mile away. They have super smelling ability. They smell prey half a mile away.

They have tiny holes around their snout. They find prey in complete darkness. They sense electricity as animals move.

Sharks have 200 teeth at a time.
They have five rows of teeth.

They feel tiny movements. They feel prey 330 feet
(100 m) away.

CONSIDER THIS!

TAKE A POSITION! There are five senses: sight, sound, taste, touch, and hearing. Which sense is the most important? Argue your point with reasons and evidence.

SAY WHAT? Reread this book. Explain how the super senses help each animal survive in its habitat. Explain how senses help humans survive.

THINK ABOUT IT! How and why do animals develop super senses? How are their senses connected to their habitats? What would happen if one of the animals featured in this book didn't have its super sense?

LEARN MORE!

- Hickman, Pamela, and Pat Stephens. *Animal Senses: How Animals See, Hear, Taste, Smell and Feel.* Toronto: Kids Can Press, 1998.
- Jenkins, Steve. *Eye to Eye: How Animals See the World.* Boston: HMH Books for Young Readers, 2014.
- Jenkins, Steve. *The Animal Book: A Collection of the Fastest, Fiercest, Toughest, Cleverest, Shyest—and Most Surprising—Animals on Earth.* Boston: HMH Books for Young Readers, 2013.

GLOSSARY

antennae (an-TEN-ee) feelers

appendages (ahp-PHEN-duh-juhz) parts of the body, like fingers

blowholes (BLOH-hohlz) nostrils on top of the heads of whales and dolphins

echolocation (ek-oh-lo-KAY-shuhn) locating system in which sounds are sent out and bounced back

faint (FAYNT) not strong

habitats (HAB-ih-tats) environments where animals live

omnivores (AHM-nuh-vorz) animals that eat both plants and meat

predators (PRED-uh-turz) hunters

prey (PRAY) animals that are hunted for food

receptors (rih-SEPT-urz) cells that sense things, feelers

sacs (SAKS) bags

savory (SAY-vur-ee) flavor that is salty and/or spicy

setae (SEE-tee) tiny hairs on body parts that feel things

snout (SNOUT) projecting nose and mouth

stalks (STAWKS) sticks

survive (sur-VIVE) to live, to stay alive

territory (TER-ih-tor-ee) area

trunk (TRUNGK) protruding body part that is a combination of a nose and upper lip

ultrasound (UHL-truh-sound) invisible sound waves

INDEX